THE EMPEROR'S SILENT ARMY

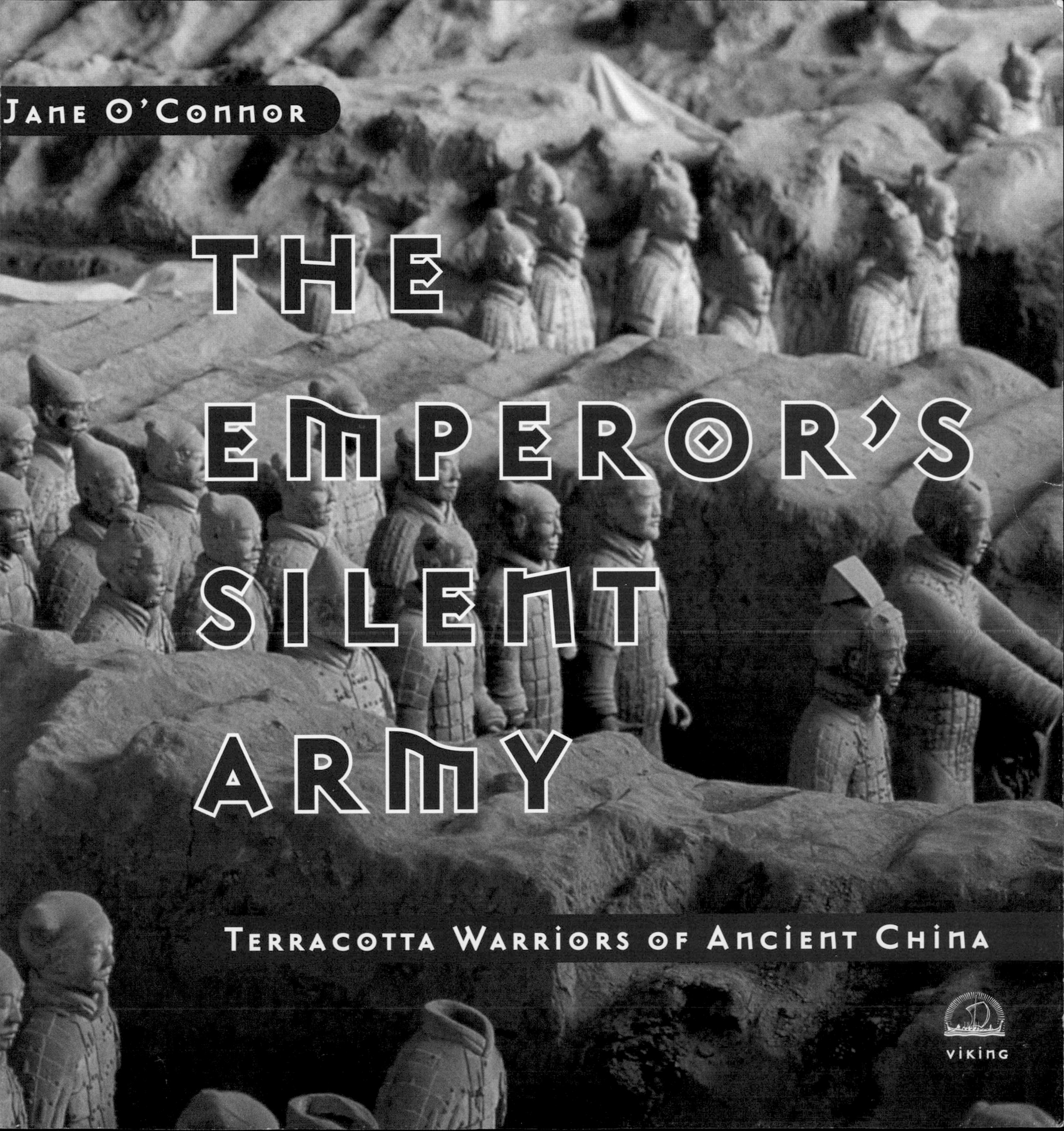

Jane O'Connor

The Emperor's Silent Army

Terracotta Warriors of Ancient China

Viking

To my sister, Jill, for going with me

I would like to thank Jerome Lacrosniere of Imaginechina.com and Beth Rae Richardson of the National Geographic Society Image Collection for all their help and patience providing photographs for this book.

VIKING
Published by the Penguin Group
Penguin Putnam Books for Young Readers, 345 Hudson Street, New York, New York 10014, U.S.A.

Penguin Books Ltd, Registered Offices: Harmondsworth, Middlesex, England

Published in 2002 by Viking, a division of Penguin Putnam Books for Young Readers.

1 3 5 7 9 10 8 6 4 2

LIBRARY OF CONGRESS CATALOGING-IN-PUBLICATION DATA
O'Connor, Jane.
The emperor's silent army : terracotta warriors of Ancient China / Jane O'Connor.
p. cm.
Includes bibliographical references and index.
Summary: Describes the archaeological discovery of thousands of life-sized terracotta warrior statues in northern China in 1974, and discusses the emperor who had them created and placed near his tomb.
ISBN 0-670-03512-2
1. Qin Shihuang, Emperor of China, 259-210 B.C.—Tomb—Juvenile literature. 2. Terra-cotta sculpture, Chinese—Ch'in-Han dynasties, 221 B.C.-220 A.D.—Juvenile literature. 3. Shaanxi Sheng (China)—Antiquities—Juvenile literature. [1. Qin Shihuang, Emperor of China, 259-210 B.C. 2. China—History—Qin dynasty, 221-207 B.C. 3. China—Antiquities. 4. Archaeology.] I. Title: Terracotta warriors of Ancient China. II. Title.
DS747.9.C47 O26 2001 931—dc21 2001046900

Printed in Hong Kong
Set in Janson

Photo credits: Front cover jacket photo: Zhou Kang/ © copyright 2001 Imaginechina.com. All rights reserved. Back cover: The Art Archive/ British Library. Title page: Wolfgang Kaehler/Getty News Sources/ Getty Images. Page 6: Zhuge Ming/ © copyright 2001 Imaginechina.com. All rights reserved. Page 8: O. Louis Mazzatenta/ National Geographic Society Image Collection. Page 9: Zhou Kang/ © copyright 2001 Imaginechina.com. All rights reserved. Pages 10-11: Zhou Kang/ © copyright 2001 Imaginechina.com. All rights reserved. Page 13: Rick Britton. Page 14: Giraudon/Art Resource, New York. Page 15: O. Louis Mazzatenta/National Geographic Society Image Collection. Page 16: Tomb of Qin Shi Huang Di, Xianyang, China/Bridgeman Art Library. Page 17: Private Collection/Bonhams, London, UK/Bridgeman Art Library. Pages 20-21: O. Louis Mazzatenta/ National Geographic Society Image Collection. Page 22: Tomb of Qin Shi Huang Di, Xianyang, China/Bridgeman Art Library. Page 23: Zhou Kang/ © copyright 2001. Imaginechina.com. All rights reserved. Page 24: O. Louis Mazzatenta/ National Geographic Society Image Collection. Page 25: The Art Archive/Dagli Orti. Page 26: O. Louis Mazzatenta/ National Geographic Society Image Collection. Page 27: O. Louis Mazzatenta/ National Geographic Society Image Collection. Page 29 top left and right, bottom right: P. Aventurier/Getty News Sources/Getty Images; bottom left: Tomb of Qin Shi Huang Di, Xianyang, China/Bridgeman Art Library. Page 30. O. Louis Mazzatenta/National Geographic Society Image Collection. Page 31 left: O. Louis Mazzatenta/National Geographic Society Image Collection; right: Doug Stern/ National Geographic Society Image Collection. Pages 32-33: Zhang Zongkun/© copyright 2001 Imaginechina.com. All rights reserved. Page 34: O. Louis Mazzatenta/National Geographic Society Image Collection. Pages 36-37: The Art Archive/Genius of China Exhibition. Page 38: The Art Archive/British Library. Page 39: Jiang Ren/Private Collection/ © copyright 2001 Imaginechina.com. All rights reserved. Page 41: Private Collection/The Stapleton Collection/Bridgeman Art Library. Pages 42-43: Jin Shi Zi/ © copyright 2001 Imaginechina.com. All rights reserved. Page 44: Giraudon/Art Resource, New York.

Contents

CHAPTER 1

A Strange Discovery

Lintong County, People's Republic of China, March 1974

IT'S just an ordinary day in early spring, or so three farmers think as they trudge across a field in northern China. They are looking for a good place to dig a well. There has been a drought, and they must find water or risk losing their crops later in the year.

The farmers choose a spot near a grove of persimmon trees. Down they dig, five feet, ten feet. Still no water. They decide to keep on digging a little deeper. All of a sudden, one of the farmers feels his shovel strike against something hard. Is it a rock? It's difficult to see at the bottom of the dark hole, so the farmer kneels down for a closer look. No, it isn't a rock. It seems to be clay, and not raw clay but clay that has been baked and made into something. But what?

Now, more carefully, the men dig around the something. Perhaps it is a pot or a vase. However, what slowly reveals itself is the pottery head of a man who stares back at them, open-eyed and amazingly real looking. The farmers have never seen anything like it before. But they do remember stories that some of the old people in

The terracotta figures were discovered in the countryside of northern China.

The terracotta army was discovered when well-diggers found the head of a "pottery man" like this one. No photographs were taken that day.

their village have told, stories of a "pottery man" found many years ago not far from where they are now. The villagers had been scared that the pottery man would bring bad luck so they broke it to bits, which were then reburied and forgotten.

The three well-diggers are not so superstitious. They report their discovery to a local official. Soon a group of archeologists arrives to search the area more closely. Maybe they will find pieces of a clay body to go with the clay head.

In fact, they find much more.

During the weeks and months that follow, the archeologists dig out more pottery men, which now are called by a more dignified term—terracotta figurines. The figurines are soldiers. That much is clear. But they come from a time long ago, when

Chinese warriors wore knee-length robes, armor made from small iron "fish scales," and elaborate topknot hairdos. All of the soldiers are life-size or a little bigger and weigh as much as four hundred pounds. They stand at attention as if waiting for the command to charge into battle. The only thing missing is their weapons. And those are found too—hundreds of real bronze swords, daggers, and battle-axes as well as thousands of scattered arrowheads—all so perfectly made that, after cleaning, their ancient tips are still sharp enough to split a hair!

Today, after nearly thirty years of work, terracotta soldiers are still being uncovered and restored. What the well-diggers stumbled upon, purely by accident, has

These soldiers' hands are clenched as if still holding their bronze weapons.

turned out to be among the largest and most incredible archeological discoveries of modern times. Along with the Great Pyramids in Egypt, the buried army is now considered one of the true wonders of the ancient world. Spread out over several acres near the city of Xian, the soldiers number not in the tens or hundreds but in the thousands! Probably 7,500 total. Until 1974, nobody knew that right below the people of northern China an enormous underground army had been standing guard, silently and watchfully, for more than 2,200 years. Who put them there?

One man.

Known as the fierce tiger of Qin, the divine Son of Heaven, he was the first emperor of China.

Although more than seven thousand strong, the terracotta army is small compared to the emperor's real army.

CHAPTER 2

The Quest for Immortality

BEFORE the time of Qin Shihuang (pronounced chin shir-hwong), who lived from 259 to 210 B.C., there was no China. Instead, there were seven separate kingdoms, each with its own language, currency, and ruler. For hundreds of years they had been fighting one another. The kingdom of Qin was the fiercest; soldiers received their pay only after they had presented their generals with the cut-off heads of enemy warriors. By 221 B.C. the ruler of the Qin kingdom had "eaten up his neighbors like a silkworm devouring a leaf," according to an ancient historian. The name China comes from Qin.

The king of Qin now ruled over an immense empire—around one million square miles that stretched north and west to the Gobi desert, south to present-day Vietnam, and east to the Yellow Sea. To the people of the time, this was the entire civilized world. Not for another hundred years would the Chinese know that empires existed beyond their boundaries. To the ruler of Qin, being called king was no longer grand enough. He wanted a title that no one else had ever had before. What he chose was Qin Shihuang. This means "first emperor, God in Heaven, and Almighty of the Universe" all rolled into one.

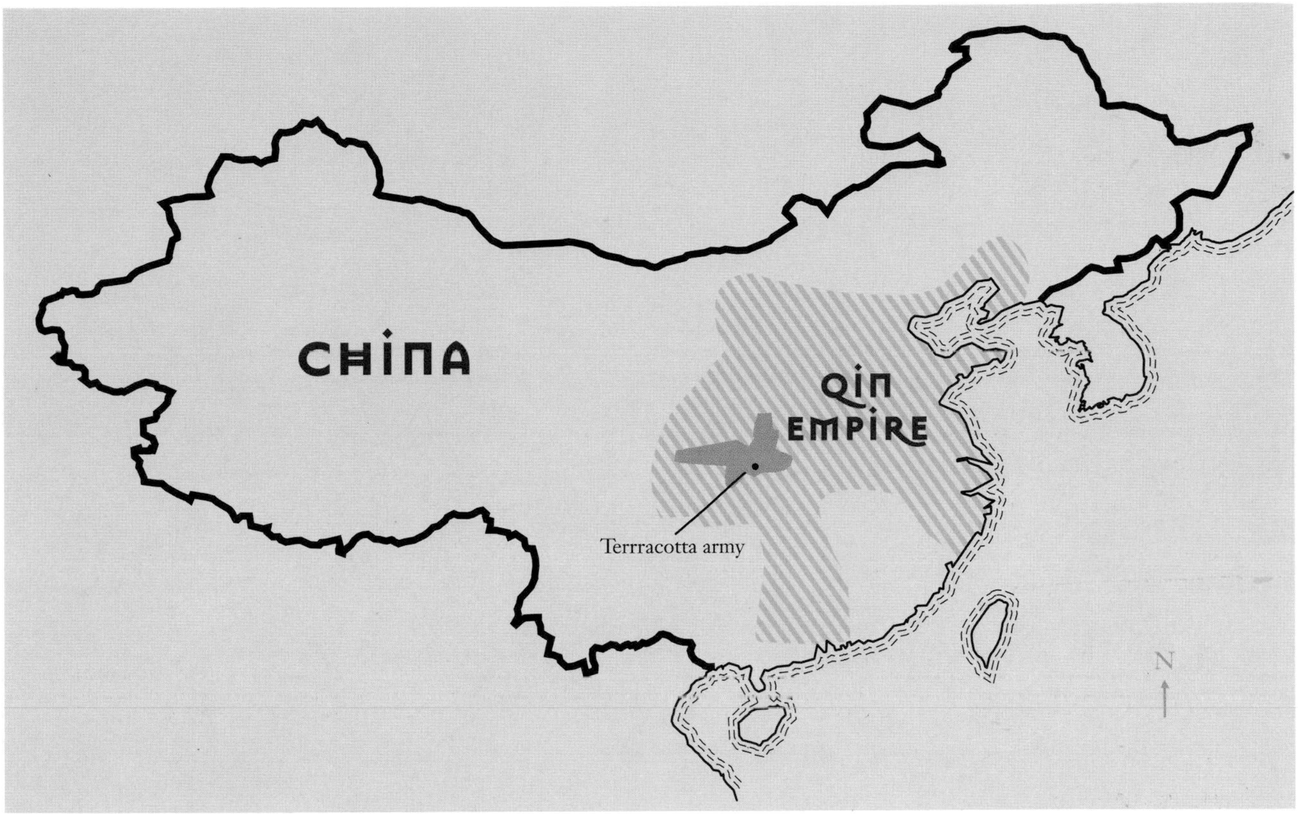

The map shows the Qin kingdom in brown and the Qin empire in stripes. The dot indicates where the terracotta army was found.

But no title, however superhuman it sounded, could protect him from what he feared most—dying. More than anything, the emperor wanted to live forever. According to legend, a magic elixir had granted eternal life to the people of the mythical Eastern Islands. Over the years, the emperor sent expeditions out to sea in search of the islands and the magic potion. But each time they came back empty-handed.

If he couldn't live forever, then Qin Shihuang was determined to live as long as possible. He ate powdered jade and drank mercury in the belief that they would prolong his life. In fact, these "medicines" were poison and may have caused the emperor to fall sick and die while on a tour of the easternmost outposts of his empire. He was forty-nine years old.

If word of Qin Shihuang's death got out while he was away from the capital there might be a revolt. So his ministers kept the news a secret. With the emperor's body inside his chariot, the entire party traveled back to the capital city. Meals were brought into the emperor's chariot; daily reports on affairs of state were delivered as usual—all to keep up the appearance that the emperor was alive and well. However, it was summer, and a terrible smell began to come from the chariot. But the clever ministers found a way to account for the stench. A cart was loaded with smelly salted fish and made to precede the chariot, overpowering and masking any foul odors

Right: This is a modern stone engraving of the first emperor of China. *Opposite page:* This painting from the seventeenth century shows the first emperor carried on a covered litter called a palanquin.

On long journeys, the emperor would have slept in a covered carriage like this half-scale model made from bronze in the third century B.C.

coming from the dead emperor. And so Qin Shihuang returned to the capital for burial.

The tomb of Qin Shihuang had been under construction for more than thirty years. It was begun when he was a young boy of thirteen and was still not finished when he died. Even incomplete, the emperor's tomb was enormous, larger than his largest palace. According to legend, it had a domed ceiling inlaid with clusters of pearls to represent the sun, moon, and stars. Below was a gigantic relief map of the world, made from bronze. Bronze hills and mountains rose up from the floor, with rivers of mercury flowing into a mercury sea. Along the banks of the rivers were models of the emperor's palaces and cities, all exact replicas of the real ones.

In ancient times, the Chinese believed that life after death was not so very different from life on earth. The soul of a dead person could continue to enjoy all the pleasures of everyday life. So people who were rich enough constructed elaborate underground tombs filled with silk robes, jewelry with precious stones, furniture, games, boats, chariots—everything the dead person could possibly need or want.

For thousands of years, the Chinese have made silk fabric. This detail of a silk robe shows an embroidered dragon, the symbol of Chinese emperors.

Qin Shihuang knew that grave robbers would try their best to loot the treasures in his tomb. So he had machines put inside the tomb that produced the rumble of thunder to scare off intruders, and mechanical crossbows at the entrance were set to fire arrows automatically should anyone dare trespass. The emperor also made certain that the workers who carried his coffin in to its final resting place never revealed its exact whereabouts. As the men worked their way back through the tunnels to the tomb's entrance, a stone door came crashing down, and they were left to die, sealed inside the tomb along with the body of the emperor.

Even all these measures, however, were not enough to satisfy the emperor. And so, less than a mile from the tomb, in underground trenches, the terracotta warriors were stationed. Just as flesh-and-blood troops had protected him during his lifetime, the terracotta troops were there to protect their ruler against any enemy for all eternity.

CHAPTER 3

Buried Soldiers

QIN Shihuang became emperor because of his stunning victories on the battlefield. His army was said to be a million strong. In every respect except for number, the terracotta army is a faithful replica of the real one.

So far terracotta troops have been found in three separate pits, all close to one another. A fourth pit was discovered, but it was empty. The entire army faces east. The Qin kingdom, the emperor's homeland, was in the northwest. The other kingdoms that had been conquered and had become part of his empire lay to the east. So Qin Shihuang feared that any enemy uprising would come from that direction.

The first pit is by far the biggest, more than two football fields long, with approximately six thousand soldiers and horses. About one thousand have already been excavated and restored. None of the soldiers in the army wears a helmet or carries a shield, proof of the Qin soldiers' fearlessness. But the archers stationed in the front lines don't wear any armor either. They needed to be able to move freely in order to fire their arrows with accuracy. And so these frontline sharpshooters, who were the first targets of an approaching enemy, also had the least protection.

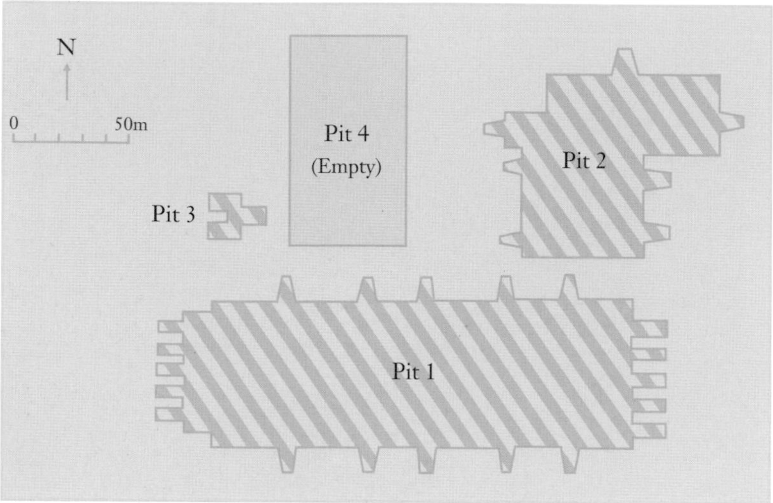

Following the vanguard are eleven long columns of foot soldiers and lower-ranking officers, the main body of the army, who once carried spears, battle-axes, and halberds. The soldiers are prepared for an attack from any direction; those in the extreme right and extreme left columns face out, not forward, so that they can block enemy charges from either side. Last of all comes the rear guard, three rows of soldiers with their backs to the rest of the army, ready to stop an attack from behind.

Above: This diagram shows the four pits that have been discovered. Only three contain terracotta figures.
Right: In Pit 1, three rows of unarmored soldiers are followed by the main body of the army.

Low-ranking infantrymen wore no armor.

Stationed at various points among the foot soldiers are about fifty charioteers who drove wooden chariots. Each charioteer has a team of four horses and is dressed in full-length armor. In some carts, a general rides beside the charioteer, ready to beat a drum to signal a charge or ring a bell to call for a retreat.

The long rectangular arrangement of soldiers in Pit 1 follows a real battle formation used to defeat real enemies in ancient times. It is called a sword formation, with the frontline archers representing the tip of the sword, the chariots and columns of foot soldiers forming the blade, and the rear guard the handle.

Pit 2 is far smaller than Pit 1. With an estimated 900 warriors of all different ranks, Pit 2 serves as a powerful back-up force to help the larger army in Pit 1. There are also almost 500 horses—about 350 chariot horses and more than 100 cavalry horses.

Right: This drawing shows what a wooden chariot would have looked like. *Below:* The actual chariots rotted away long before the discovery of the terracotta army.

The terracotta horses are Mongolian ponies, not very big, but muscular and full of power. With their flaring nostrils, bared teeth, and bulging eyes, the chariot horses all look as if they are straining to gallop across a battlefield. The mane of each chariot horse is trimmed short and its tail is braided. That is so it won't get caught in the harness.

The terracotta horses are life-size.

A cavalry officer with his horse.

By the time of the first emperor, soldiers on horseback were replacing war chariots. It was hard for even the most experienced drivers to manage a chariot over bumpy, rock-strewn ground. Cavalrymen could move much more swiftly and easily. Their horses had fancy saddles decorated with rows of nail heads and tassels, but no stirrups—they hadn't come into use yet.

Pit 3, by far the smallest, contains fewer than seventy warriors and only one team of horses. Archeologists think that Pit 3 represents army headquarters. That's because the soldiers are not arranged in an attack formation.

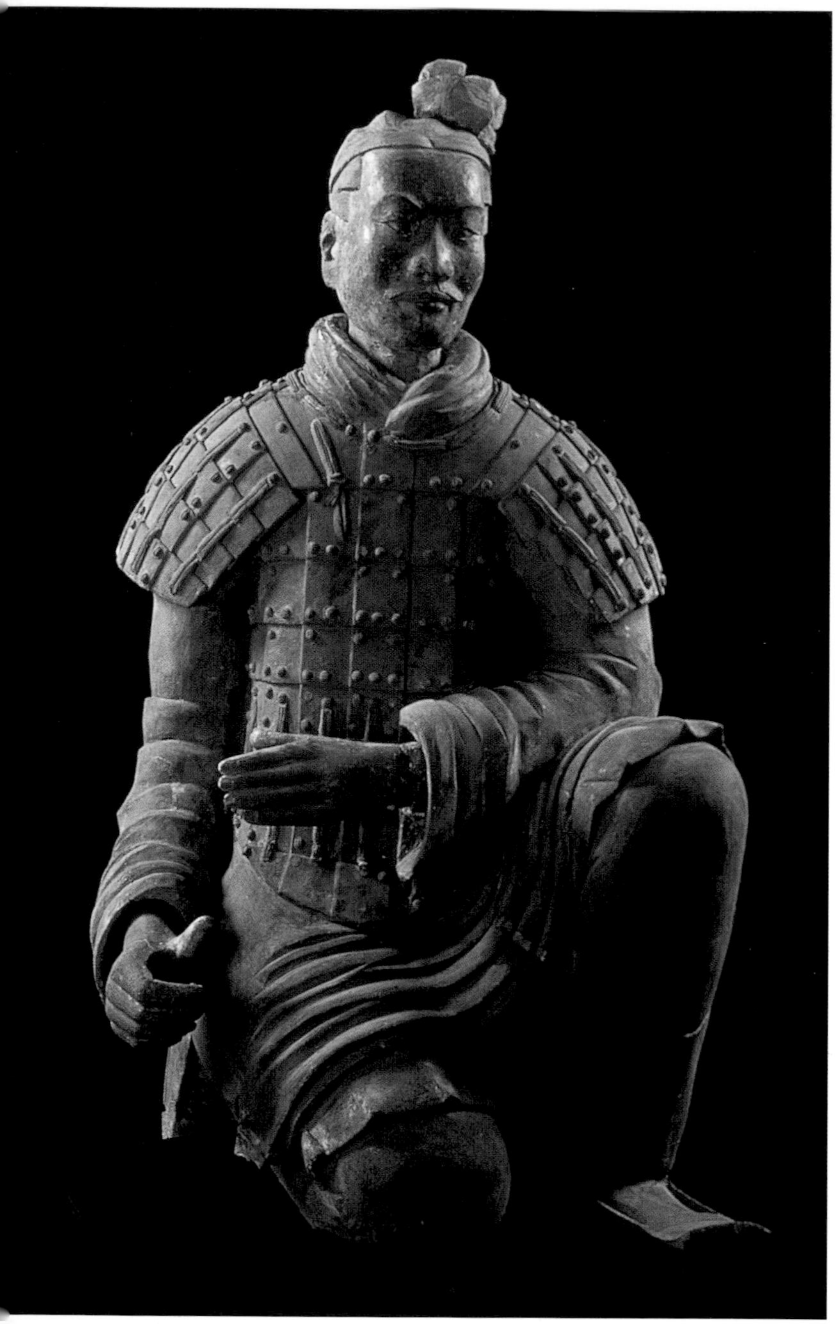

Instead, they face one another in a U shape, as if they are busy consulting among themselves. Although the officers at command central would not engage in hand-to-hand combat, the fate of the thousands of troops in Pit 1 and Pit 2 rests in their hands.

Altogether, the three pits of warriors and horses make up an unstoppable army. All the warriors are stationed strategically, exactly as they would have been on a real battlefield. For example, rows of kneeling soldiers with crossbows alternate with rows of standing archers. This way, while one row is firing, the other row has time to reload their bows. The crossbow was by far the most powerful weapon of the time. The Chinese were using crossbows as early as 400 B.C. In Europe, however, crossbows didn't come into use for at least another 1,300 years.

This kneeling archer was found positioned in front of standing soldiers, just as he would have been on a real battlefield.

In earlier times in ancient China, real soldiers and horses were killed and buried alongside their dead ruler. But by the time of Qin Shihuang this horrible custom was no longer so common. Instead, clay or wooden figurines were substituted for human sacrifices. Once the figures were buried underground, it was believed that they would come to life magically and protect the dead emperor both from real attackers hoping to ransack his tomb and from any evil spirits wanting to harm his immortal soul.

Interestingly, there is not a single word about the buried army in any records from ancient times. Why was this? Was the creation of the clay soldiers simply not worthy of mention? Or was the emperor making sure that nobody knew about his ultimate secret weapon?

Unlike most of the figures, who stand stiffly, face forward, this archer is in a much more natural pose.

CHAPTER 4

The Faces of Ancient China

ABOUT two thousand soldiers have been unearthed, yet, amazingly, so far no two are the same. The army includes men of all different ages, from different parts of China, with different temperaments. A young soldier looks both excited and nervous; an older officer, perhaps a veteran of many wars, appears tired, resigned. Some soldiers seem lost in thought, possibly dreaming of their return home; others look proud and confident. Although from a distance the figures appear almost identical, like giant-size toy soldiers, each is a distinct work of art.

Did real-life models pose for the figures? Probably not. But hundreds of craftsmen from all over the empire spent more than ten years in workshops set up near the pits creating the warriors. It is likely that they made the faces of the soldiers look like the faces of people that they knew from home.

The uniforms of the terracotta figures are exact copies in clay of what real soldiers of the day wore. The soldier's uniform tells his rank in the army. The lowest-ranking soldiers are bareheaded and wear heavy knee-length tunics but no armor. Often their legs are wrapped in cloth shin guards for protection.

The expressions on the soldiers' faces are what makes the figures look so real.

At the time of the first emperor, Chinese men wore their waist-length hair in a variety of braids and buns.

The generals' uniforms are the most elegant. Their caps sometimes sport a pheasant feather; their fancy shoes curl up at the toes; and their fine armor is made from small iron fish scales. Tassels on their armor are also a mark of their high rank.

The terracotta soldiers are now the ghostly grayish color of baked clay, clay that came from nearby Mount Li. Originally the soldiers were all brightly colored. Tiny bits of paint can still be seen on many of the figures and are proof that uniforms came in a blaze of colors—purple, blue, green, yellow, red, and orange. The colors of each soldier's uniform indicated not only which part of the army he belonged to—cavalry or infantry, for example—but also what his particular rank was. The terracotta horses were fully painted, too, in brown with pink ears, nostrils, and mouths. Unfortunately, when figures are dug out of the ground, most of the paint on them peels off and sticks to the surrounding earth. Also, when exposed to air, the paint tends to crumble into dust.

The colored computer image shows how the general would have looked originally.

Modern-day potters make replicas of soldiers, faithfully copying every detail of their uniforms.

Today groups of artisans in workshops near the three pits make replicas of the soldiers, following the techniques used 2,200 years ago. Their work helps archeologists learn more about how the original figures were created. Even though the workers today have the advantages of modern kilns that register temperatures exactly, no copies have ever come out as hard or as lustrous as the ancient originals. (The workers of today are also not under the same kind of pressure as the emperor's potters—if they made a mistake, they were killed!)

Who were the potters who made the original soldiers? For the most part, they have remained anonymous. In ancient times, being a craftsman was considered lowly work. However, some soldiers are signed, probably by the master potter in charge of a workshop. The signature is like a stamp of approval, a sign of quality control.

Of course, the creators of the terracotta warriors never intended their work to be seen by anyone other than the emperor. That is a strange notion for twenty-first-century minds to accept. Artists today want their work to be seen, enjoyed, admired. But as soon as the emperor's army was completed, it was buried. Pits were dug twenty feet deep. Green-tiled floors were laid down. Dirt walls were constructed, creating tunnels in which the soldiers and horses and chariots were placed. A wooden roof was built overhead, and then ten feet of dirt was shoveled on top of the army. It was supposed to remain undisturbed for all eternity, but it did not turn out that way. How surprised the Qin sculptors would be by the crowds of people from all over the world who come to see their creations!

This cross-section drawing shows how the soldiers in Pit 1 were placed in underground tunnels, which were separated by earthen walls and covered by a wooden roof.

‡ CHAPTER 5 ‡

Inside the Emperor's Tomb

WHAT exactly is the terracotta army guarding so steadfastly? What, besides the body of the dead emperor, is inside the tomb? The answer is that nobody knows. And the government of China has no plans at present to excavate and find out.

In ancient China it was the custom to build a natural-looking hill on top of a person's tomb. The more important a person was, the bigger the hill. Thousands

of years of harsh weather have worn down the emperor's mound; originally it was four hundred feet high, almost as high as the biggest of the three Great Pyramids in Egypt.

Like the ancient Egyptians, the ancient Chinese believed that the body of a dead person should be preserved as a "home" for the soul. However, the Chinese did not make a person's body into a mummy. They believed that jade had magic powers, among them the ability to keep a dead body from decaying. In Chinese tombs from the first century B.C., bodies of noblemen and princesses have been found wearing entire suits of jade. It is believed that Qin Shihuang is buried in just

The body of the emperor, which has never been uncovered, may wear a jade funeral suit like this one found in the tomb of a Chinese princess from the late second century.

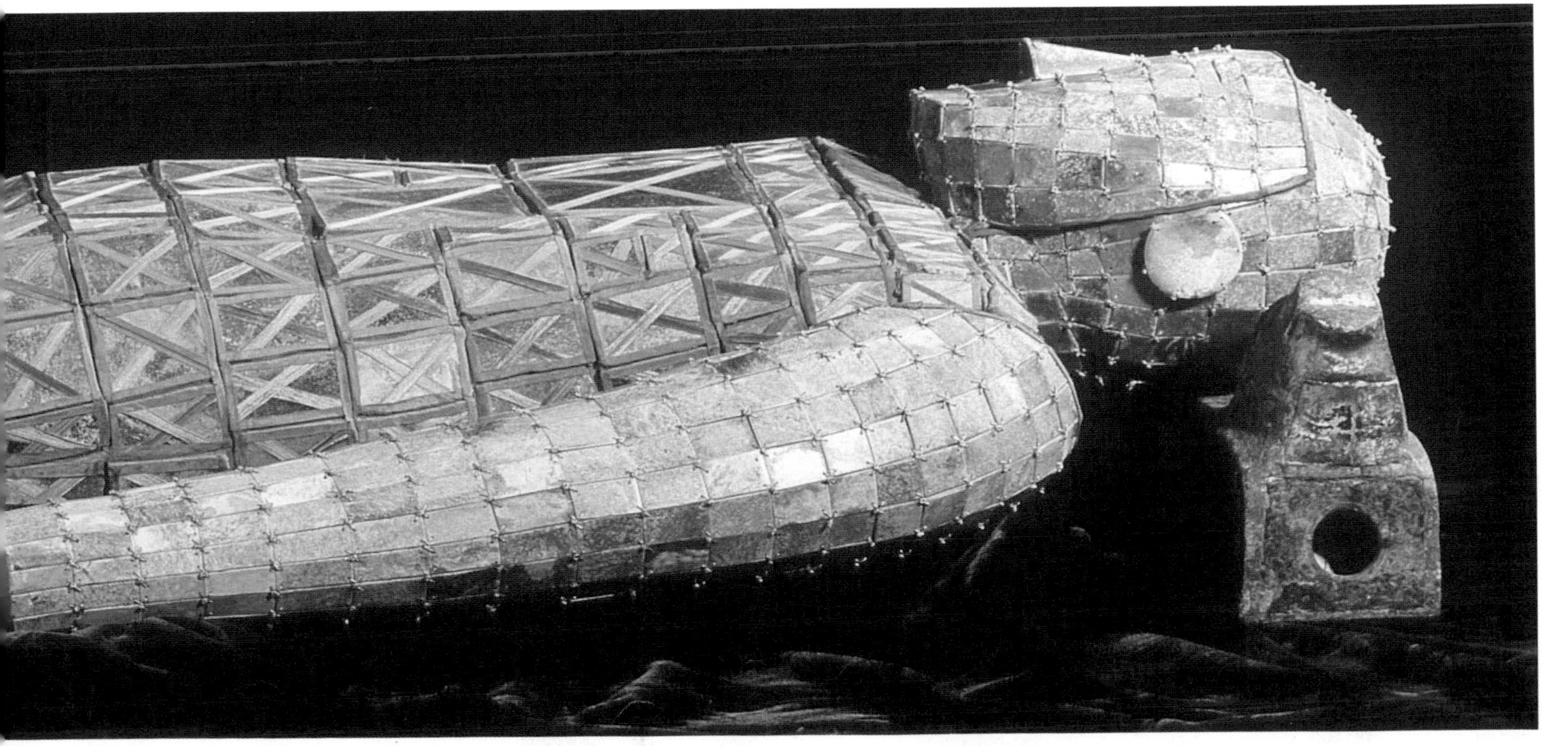

No paintings exist of the emperor done in his lifetime, so there is no way to know how faithful this portrait is.

such a suit, the thousands of small tiles all beautifully carved and sewn together with gold thread. And over this jade burial outfit, his body is supposedly covered in a blanket of pearls.

As for all the things placed with the emperor, certainly they must be grand beyond imagining—silk robes embroidered with dragons, gem-encrusted crowns and jewelry, musical instruments, hand-carved furniture, lamps, beautiful dishes, cooking pots, and golden utensils. Like the pharaohs of ancient Egypt, the first emperor would have made certain that he had everything he might possibly want in the afterlife. But unless his tomb is excavated, what these treasures look like will remain a mystery.

Beautiful silk robes, like this one from the nineteenth century, would be placed in the tomb of an important person to be worn in the afterlife.

CHAPTER 6

The Emperor's Legacy

THE first emperor was in power for only eleven years. But in that brief time, he created a unified country out of all the warring kingdoms that he had conquered. Qin Shihuang built four thousand miles of roads that connected all parts of his huge empire. Instead of many different written languages, he decreed that there would be just one, just as there would be only one kind of currency and one system of weights and measures.

Qin Shihuang wanted to protect his new empire from barbarian tribes. So he built the first Great Wall of China. There already were many small walls scattered across the northwest frontier. The emperor had these walls joined together to create 1,500 miles of fortification.

With a workforce of half a million slave laborers, it took only twelve years to build the wall. It was an amazing feat; to this day, it remains the longest man-made structure in the world. But the wall was also built at a tremendous cost in terms of human suffering. During its construction, it was called "the longest cemetery on earth" because so many thousands of men died building it.

Qin Shihuang built the first Great Wall of China, pictured here in an eighteenth-century painting.

Qin Shihuang was a tyrant, ruthless and cruel, and one of the most despised rulers in China's long history. He believed that people were evil by nature. And he believed that ignorant people were easier to control than educated ones. So at his command all books were burned, except for ones on medicine and farming, since those subjects were unlikely to put dangerous ideas in people's heads. What exactly were dangerous ideas? Any that went against his own. Qin Shihuang silenced 460 scholars who were critical of him by burying them alive in a common grave.

Although he died a natural death, there had been at least three attempts to assassinate him. The emperor had 270 palaces and he moved from one to another constantly, never spending two nights in the same place. He went out only at night and only in disguise, so great was his fear of plots to kill him.

Qin Shihuang boasted that his descendants would rule China for ten thousand generations. However, his royal family, or dynasty,

Today the Great Wall snakes across northern China; none of the sections built during the time of the first emperor still stands.

坑儒焚書

stayed in power barely beyond his own lifetime. After his death in 210 B.C., one of his twenty sons took the throne. Then just three years later, there was a peasant rebellion. One of its leaders became emperor, beginning a new dynasty—the Han dynasty—that ruled China for the next four hundred years. Still, the empire that Qin Shihuang created lasted for more than two thousand years. Until 1912, China was ruled by an emperor, each, like Qin Shihuang, considered all-powerful and godlike.

The rebels who brought an end to the Qin dynasty killed troops loyal to the emperor. They also did their best to destroy the underground clay army. The peasant soldiers stormed the entrances to the pits, snatched up bronze weapons, and set fire to the wooden roofs, which collapsed on the soldiers and horses, smashing most to bits.

For centuries after that, the world forgot about the buried, broken army of clay . . . until that day in 1974. More than anything, Qin Shihuang wanted immortality. Now, each year more than two million people from all over the world come to his burial site to see his army. So, perhaps, in some way, the emperor has lived on.

In this painting, the first emperor, in white robes, watches the book burning and the massacre of scholars who were critical of him.

‡ Author's Note ‡

In January 2000, I went to Xian to "inspect" the terracotta troops. It was an overwhelming experience, and since that time I have read whatever I could find on the clay army as well as on the emperor who ordered its creation.

The more I read, the more I saw how hard it was to separate fact from legend. Much of what is known about Qin Shihuang comes from a single historian, a man named Sima Qian. But Sima Qian was born about sixty-five years after the emperor died. He was not writing about a time that he had lived through, so none of his information was firsthand—it all came from legends and stories passed down from an earlier era. And since no one who actually saw the inside of the emperor's tomb lived to tell about it, all of the amazing "facts"—the miniature bronze palaces, the gem-encrusted ceiling, the rivers of mercury—were never more than hearsay.

As for the terracotta army, no mention of it appears in any record from ancient times. Its discovery came as a complete surprise to the modern world. And although much has been written since the discovery of the first pit in 1974, even being accurate about relatively recent events was difficult. During the 1970s, the People's Republic of China was cut off from the rest of the world; the release of information was strictly controlled. Many of the books I had about the terracotta army were English translations of books originally published in Chinese. How accurate were the translations? Often answers varied even to the most basic questions: for example, exactly what pieces of soldiers did the well-diggers first find? At times, I had to rely on what seemed most logical to me or on the books that seemed the most carefully researched and trustworthy.

Ultimately, I came to accept the contradictions and what was unknowable. Somehow this added to the mystery of the emperor and his army. I liked that the story was open-ended. Just as more figures will be unearthed, new information about this fascinating place and time will come to light.

Jane O'Connor
New York, 2001

‡ Bibliography ‡

Cotterell, Arthur. *Ancient China*. New York: Dorling Kindersley, 1994.

____________. *The First Emperor of China: The Story Behind the Terracotta Army of Mount Li*. New York: Penguin Books, 1988.

Cottrell, Leonard. *The Tiger of Qin: The Dramatic Emergence of China as a Nation*. New York: Holt, Rinehart and Winston, 1962.

Debaine-Francfort, Corinne. *The Search for Ancient China*. New York: Harry N. Abrams, Inc., 1999.

Fairbank, John King, and Merle Goldman. *China: A New History*. Cambridge, Mass.: The Belknap Press of Harvard University Press, 1998.

Fu Tianchou, ed. *The Underground Terracotta Army of Emperor Qin Shi Huang*. Beijing: New World Press, 1985.

Haw, Stephen G. *A Traveller's History of China*. 2d ed. New York: Interlink Publishing, 1998.

Huang, Ray. *China: A Macro History*. n.p.: M. E. Sharpe, Inc., 1990

Lei Congyun, Yang Yang, and Zhao Gushan. *Imperial Tombs of China*. Memphis, Tenn.: Wonders, 1995.

Mazzatenta, O. Louis. "China's Warriors Rise from the Earth," *National Geographic Magazine*, vol. 190, no. 4 (October 1996), pp. 68–80.

Siliotti, Alberto. *Dwellings of Eternity*. New York: Barnes and Noble, 2000.

Steele, Philip. *Step into the Chinese Empire*. Boston: Little Brown, 1998.

Topping, Audrey. "China's Incredible Find: The First Emperor's Army," *National Geographic Magazine*, vol. 153, no. 4 (April 1978), pp. 440–59.

Williams, Brian. *See Through History: Ancient China*. New York: Viking Books, 1996.

Wu Xiaocong. *The Subterranean Army of Emperor Qin Shi Huang*. Beijing: China Travel and Tourism Press, 1999.

Xiaoneng Yang, ed. *The Golden Age of Chinese Archaeology: Celebrated Discoveries from the People's Republic of China*. Washington, D.C.: National Gallery of Art, 1999.

Zhang Wenli. *The Qin Terra Cotta Army: Treasures of Lintong*. Beijing: Scala Books/Cultural Relics Publishing House, 1996.

Index